This planner belongs to:

_____

Weekly PLANNER

MONDAY	TUESDAY	WEDNESDAY	THURSDAY

TO DO LIST:

☐
☐
☐
☐
☐
☐
☐
☐
☐
☐
☐
☐

APPOINTMENTS:

SPECIAL EVENTS:

SELF CARE AND HABIT TRACKER:

		M	T	W	T	F	S	S
		M	T	W	T	F	S	S
		M	T	W	T	F	S	S
		M	T	W	T	F	S	S
		M	T	W	T	F	S	S
		M	T	W	T	F	S	S
		M	T	W	T	F	S	S
		M	T	W	T	F	S	S

WEEK OF: ....

FRIDAY	SATURDAY	SUNDAY	REFLECTIONS:

WEEKLY GOALS:

ACTION PLAN:

MOTIVATION:

AFFIRMATIONS:

NOTES:

NEXT WEEK:

Power HOUR

DATE: ....

TOP PRIORITIES:

CALLS & CHECK-INS

FOLLOW-UPS

FIND NEW LEADS

CORRESPONDENCES

SOCIAL MEDIA POSTS

DATE: ....

TOP PRIORITIES:

CALLS & CHECK-INS

FOLLOW-UPS

FIND NEW LEADS

CORRESPONDENCES

SOCIAL MEDIA POSTS

Sales & Expense TRACKER

DATE	CUSTOMER	PRODUCT	QTY	AMOUNT	NOTES	✓

DATE	EXPENSE DESCRIPTION	AMOUNT	✓

Downline DEVELOPMENT

NAME:	DATE:

GOALS:

ACHIEVEMENTS:

FOCUS AREAS:

MOTIVATION:

NEXT MEETING:

NOTES:

NAME:	DATE:

GOALS:

ACHIEVEMENTS:

FOCUS AREAS:

MOTIVATION:

NEXT MEETING:

NOTES:

NAME:	DATE:

GOALS:

ACHIEVEMENTS:

FOCUS AREAS:

MOTIVATION:

NEXT MEETING:

NOTES:

Recruiting POTENTIALS

NAME:	FOLLOW-UP DATE:
THEIR WHY:	
WHAT'S THE HOLD-UP:	
HOW CAN I HELP:	
NOTES:	

NAME:	FOLLOW-UP DATE:
THEIR WHY:	
WHAT'S THE HOLD-UP:	
HOW CAN I HELP:	
NOTES:	

NAME:	FOLLOW-UP DATE:
THEIR WHY:	
WHAT'S THE HOLD-UP:	
HOW CAN I HELP:	
NOTES:	

NAME:	FOLLOW-UP DATE:
THEIR WHY:	
WHAT'S THE HOLD-UP:	
HOW CAN I HELP:	
NOTES:	

NAME:	FOLLOW-UP DATE:
THEIR WHY:	
WHAT'S THE HOLD-UP:	
HOW CAN I HELP:	
NOTES:	

Weekly PLANNER

MONDAY	TUESDAY	WEDNESDAY	THURSDAY

TO DO LIST:

- ☐
- ☐
- ☐
- ☐
- ☐
- ☐
- ☐
- ☐
- ☐
- ☐
- ☐
- ☐

APPOINTMENTS:

SPECIAL EVENTS:

SELF CARE AND HABIT TRACKER:

	M	T	W	T	F	S	S
	M	T	W	T	F	S	S
	M	T	W	T	F	S	S
	M	T	W	T	F	S	S
	M	T	W	T	F	S	S
	M	T	W	T	F	S	S
	M	T	W	T	F	S	S
	M	T	W	T	F	S	S

WEEK OF:

FRIDAY	SATURDAY	SUNDAY	REFLECTIONS:

WEEKLY GOALS:

ACTION PLAN:

MOTIVATION:

AFFIRMATIONS:

NOTES:

NEXT WEEK:

Power HOUR

DATE: ....

DATE: ....

TOP PRIORITIES:

TOP PRIORITIES:

CALLS & CHECK-INS

CALLS & CHECK-INS

FOLLOW-UPS

FOLLOW-UPS

FIND NEW LEADS

FIND NEW LEADS

CORRESPONDENCES

CORRESPONDENCES

SOCIAL MEDIA POSTS

SOCIAL MEDIA POSTS

Sales & Expense TRACKER

DATE	CUSTOMER	PRODUCT	QTY	AMOUNT	NOTES	✓

DATE	EXPENSE DESCRIPTION	AMOUNT	✓

Downline DEVELOPMENT

NAME:	DATE:

GOALS:

ACHIEVEMENTS:

FOCUS AREAS:

MOTIVATION:

NEXT MEETING:

NOTES:

NAME:	DATE:

GOALS:

ACHIEVEMENTS:

FOCUS AREAS:

MOTIVATION:

NEXT MEETING:

NOTES:

NAME:	DATE:

GOALS:

ACHIEVEMENTS:

FOCUS AREAS:

MOTIVATION:

NEXT MEETING:

NOTES:

Recruiting POTENTIALS

NAME:	FOLLOW-UP DATE:
THEIR WHY:	
WHAT'S THE HOLD-UP:	
HOW CAN I HELP:	
NOTES:	

NAME:	FOLLOW-UP DATE:
THEIR WHY:	
WHAT'S THE HOLD-UP:	
HOW CAN I HELP:	
NOTES:	

NAME:	FOLLOW-UP DATE:
THEIR WHY:	
WHAT'S THE HOLD-UP:	
HOW CAN I HELP:	
NOTES:	

NAME:	FOLLOW-UP DATE:
THEIR WHY:	
WHAT'S THE HOLD-UP:	
HOW CAN I HELP:	
NOTES:	

NAME:	FOLLOW-UP DATE:
THEIR WHY:	
WHAT'S THE HOLD-UP:	
HOW CAN I HELP:	
NOTES:	

Weekly PLANNER

MONDAY	TUESDAY	WEDNESDAY	THURSDAY

TO DO LIST:

- ☐
- ☐
- ☐
- ☐
- ☐
- ☐
- ☐
- ☐
- ☐
- ☐
- ☐
- ☐

APPOINTMENTS:

SPECIAL EVENTS:

SELF CARE AND HABIT TRACKER:

	M	T	W	T	F	S	S
	M	T	W	T	F	S	S
	M	T	W	T	F	S	S
	M	T	W	T	F	S	S
	M	T	W	T	F	S	S
	M	T	W	T	F	S	S
	M	T	W	T	F	S	S
	M	T	W	T	F	S	S

WEEK OF: ....

FRIDAY	SATURDAY	SUNDAY	REFLECTIONS:

WEEKLY GOALS:

ACTION PLAN:

MOTIVATION:

AFFIRMATIONS:

NOTES:

NEXT WEEK:

Power HOUR

DATE: ....

DATE: ....

TOP PRIORITIES:

TOP PRIORITIES:

CALLS & CHECK-INS

CALLS & CHECK-INS

FOLLOW-UPS

FOLLOW-UPS

FIND NEW LEADS

FIND NEW LEADS

CORRESPONDENCES

CORRESPONDENCES

SOCIAL MEDIA POSTS

SOCIAL MEDIA POSTS

Sales & Expense TRACKER

DATE	CUSTOMER	PRODUCT	QTY	AMOUNT	NOTES	✓

DATE	EXPENSE DESCRIPTION	AMOUNT	✓

Downline DEVELOPMENT

NAME:	DATE:

GOALS:

ACHIEVEMENTS:

FOCUS AREAS:

MOTIVATION:

NEXT MEETING:

NOTES:

NAME:	DATE:

GOALS:

ACHIEVEMENTS:

FOCUS AREAS:

MOTIVATION:

NEXT MEETING:

NOTES:

NAME:	DATE:

GOALS:

ACHIEVEMENTS:

FOCUS AREAS:

MOTIVATION:

NEXT MEETING:

NOTES:

Recruiting POTENTIALS

NAME: | **FOLLOW-UP DATE:**

THEIR WHY:

WHAT'S THE HOLD-UP:

HOW CAN I HELP:

NOTES:

NAME: | **FOLLOW-UP DATE:**

THEIR WHY:

WHAT'S THE HOLD-UP:

HOW CAN I HELP:

NOTES:

NAME: | **FOLLOW-UP DATE:**

THEIR WHY:

WHAT'S THE HOLD-UP:

HOW CAN I HELP:

NOTES:

NAME: | **FOLLOW-UP DATE:**

THEIR WHY:

WHAT'S THE HOLD-UP:

HOW CAN I HELP:

NOTES:

NAME: | **FOLLOW-UP DATE:**

THEIR WHY:

WHAT'S THE HOLD-UP:

HOW CAN I HELP:

NOTES:

Weekly PLANNER

MONDAY	TUESDAY	WEDNESDAY	THURSDAY

TO DO LIST:

- ☐
- ☐
- ☐
- ☐
- ☐
- ☐
- ☐
- ☐
- ☐
- ☐
- ☐
- ☐

APPOINTMENTS:

SPECIAL EVENTS:

SELF CARE AND HABIT TRACKER:

	M	T	W	T	F	S	S
	M	T	W	T	F	S	S
	M	T	W	T	F	S	S
	M	T	W	T	F	S	S
	M	T	W	T	F	S	S
	M	T	W	T	F	S	S
	M	T	W	T	F	S	S
	M	T	W	T	F	S	S
	M	T	W	T	F	S	S

WEEK OF: ....

FRIDAY	SATURDAY	SUNDAY	REFLECTIONS:

WEEKLY GOALS:

ACTION PLAN:

MOTIVATION:

AFFIRMATIONS:

NOTES:

NEXT WEEK:

Power HOUR

DATE: ....

DATE: ....

TOP PRIORITIES:

TOP PRIORITIES:

CALLS & CHECK-INS

CALLS & CHECK-INS

FOLLOW-UPS

FOLLOW-UPS

FIND NEW LEADS

FIND NEW LEADS

CORRESPONDENCES

CORRESPONDENCES

SOCIAL MEDIA POSTS

SOCIAL MEDIA POSTS

Sales & Expense TRACKER

DATE	CUSTOMER	PRODUCT	QTY	AMOUNT	NOTES	✓

DATE	EXPENSE DESCRIPTION	AMOUNT	✓

Downline DEVELOPMENT

NAME:	DATE:

GOALS:

ACHIEVEMENTS:

FOCUS AREAS:

MOTIVATION:

NEXT MEETING:

NOTES:

NAME:	DATE:

GOALS:

ACHIEVEMENTS:

FOCUS AREAS:

MOTIVATION:

NEXT MEETING:

NOTES:

NAME:	DATE:

GOALS:

ACHIEVEMENTS:

FOCUS AREAS:

MOTIVATION:

NEXT MEETING:

NOTES:

Recruiting POTENTIALS

NAME:	FOLLOW-UP DATE:
THEIR WHY:	
WHAT'S THE HOLD-UP:	
HOW CAN I HELP:	
NOTES:	

NAME:	FOLLOW-UP DATE:
THEIR WHY:	
WHAT'S THE HOLD-UP:	
HOW CAN I HELP:	
NOTES:	

NAME:	FOLLOW-UP DATE:
THEIR WHY:	
WHAT'S THE HOLD-UP:	
HOW CAN I HELP:	
NOTES:	

NAME:	FOLLOW-UP DATE:
THEIR WHY:	
WHAT'S THE HOLD-UP:	
HOW CAN I HELP:	
NOTES:	

NAME:	FOLLOW-UP DATE:
THEIR WHY:	
WHAT'S THE HOLD-UP:	
HOW CAN I HELP:	
NOTES:	

Weekly PLANNER

MONDAY	TUESDAY	WEDNESDAY	THURSDAY

TO DO LIST:

- ☐
- ☐
- ☐
- ☐
- ☐
- ☐
- ☐
- ☐
- ☐
- ☐
- ☐
- ☐

APPOINTMENTS:

SPECIAL EVENTS:

SELF CARE AND HABIT TRACKER:

	M	T	W	T	F	S	S
	M	T	W	T	F	S	S
	M	T	W	T	F	S	S
	M	T	W	T	F	S	S
	M	T	W	T	F	S	S
	M	T	W	T	F	S	S
	M	T	W	T	F	S	S
	M	T	W	T	F	S	S

WEEK OF: ....

FRIDAY	SATURDAY	SUNDAY	REFLECTIONS:

WEEKLY GOALS:

ACTION PLAN:

MOTIVATION:

AFFIRMATIONS:

NOTES:

NEXT WEEK:

Power HOUR

DATE: ....

TOP PRIORITIES:

DATE: ....

TOP PRIORITIES:

CALLS & CHECK-INS

CALLS & CHECK-INS

FOLLOW-UPS

FOLLOW-UPS

FIND NEW LEADS

FIND NEW LEADS

CORRESPONDENCES

CORRESPONDENCES

SOCIAL MEDIA POSTS

SOCIAL MEDIA POSTS

Sales & Expense TRACKER

DATE	CUSTOMER	PRODUCT	QTY	AMOUNT	NOTES	✓

DATE	EXPENSE DESCRIPTION	AMOUNT	✓

Downline DEVELOPMENT

NAME: | **DATE:**

GOALS:

ACHIEVEMENTS:

FOCUS AREAS:

MOTIVATION:

NEXT MEETING:

NOTES:

NAME: | **DATE:**

GOALS:

ACHIEVEMENTS:

FOCUS AREAS:

MOTIVATION:

NEXT MEETING:

NOTES:

NAME: | **DATE:**

GOALS:

ACHIEVEMENTS:

FOCUS AREAS:

MOTIVATION:

NEXT MEETING:

NOTES:

Recruiting POTENTIALS

NAME:	FOLLOW-UP DATE:
THEIR WHY:	
WHAT'S THE HOLD-UP:	
HOW CAN I HELP:	
NOTES:	

NAME:	FOLLOW-UP DATE:
THEIR WHY:	
WHAT'S THE HOLD-UP:	
HOW CAN I HELP:	
NOTES:	

NAME:	FOLLOW-UP DATE:
THEIR WHY:	
WHAT'S THE HOLD-UP:	
HOW CAN I HELP:	
NOTES:	

NAME:	FOLLOW-UP DATE:
THEIR WHY:	
WHAT'S THE HOLD-UP:	
HOW CAN I HELP:	
NOTES:	

NAME:	FOLLOW-UP DATE:
THEIR WHY:	
WHAT'S THE HOLD-UP:	
HOW CAN I HELP:	
NOTES:	

Weekly PLANNER

MONDAY	TUESDAY	WEDNESDAY	THURSDAY

TO DO LIST:

- ☐
- ☐
- ☐
- ☐
- ☐
- ☐
- ☐
- ☐
- ☐
- ☐
- ☐
- ☐

APPOINTMENTS:

SPECIAL EVENTS:

SELF CARE AND HABIT TRACKER:

	M	T	W	T	F	S	S
	☐	☐	☐	☐	☐	☐	☐
	☐	☐	☐	☐	☐	☐	☐
	☐	☐	☐	☐	☐	☐	☐
	☐	☐	☐	☐	☐	☐	☐
	☐	☐	☐	☐	☐	☐	☐
	☐	☐	☐	☐	☐	☐	☐
	☐	☐	☐	☐	☐	☐	☐
	☐	☐	☐	☐	☐	☐	☐

WEEK OF:

FRIDAY	SATURDAY	SUNDAY	REFLECTIONS:

WEEKLY GOALS:

ACTION PLAN:

MOTIVATION:

AFFIRMATIONS:

NOTES:

NEXT WEEK:

Power HOUR

DATE: ....

TOP PRIORITIES:

DATE: ....

TOP PRIORITIES:

CALLS & CHECK-INS

CALLS & CHECK-INS

FOLLOW-UPS

FOLLOW-UPS

FIND NEW LEADS

FIND NEW LEADS

CORRESPONDENCES

CORRESPONDENCES

SOCIAL MEDIA POSTS

SOCIAL MEDIA POSTS

Sales & Expense TRACKER

DATE	CUSTOMER	PRODUCT	QTY	AMOUNT	NOTES	✓

DATE	EXPENSE DESCRIPTION	AMOUNT	✓

Downline DEVELOPMENT

NAME:	DATE:

GOALS:

ACHIEVEMENTS:

FOCUS AREAS:

MOTIVATION:

NEXT MEETING:

NOTES:

NAME:	DATE:

GOALS:

ACHIEVEMENTS:

FOCUS AREAS:

MOTIVATION:

NEXT MEETING:

NOTES:

NAME:	DATE:

GOALS:

ACHIEVEMENTS:

FOCUS AREAS:

MOTIVATION:

NEXT MEETING:

NOTES:

Recruiting POTENTIALS

NAME:	FOLLOW-UP DATE:
THEIR WHY:	
WHAT'S THE HOLD-UP:	
HOW CAN I HELP:	
NOTES:	

NAME:	FOLLOW-UP DATE:
THEIR WHY:	
WHAT'S THE HOLD-UP:	
HOW CAN I HELP:	
NOTES:	

NAME:	FOLLOW-UP DATE:
THEIR WHY:	
WHAT'S THE HOLD-UP:	
HOW CAN I HELP:	
NOTES:	

NAME:	FOLLOW-UP DATE:
THEIR WHY:	
WHAT'S THE HOLD-UP:	
HOW CAN I HELP:	
NOTES:	

NAME:	FOLLOW-UP DATE:
THEIR WHY:	
WHAT'S THE HOLD-UP:	
HOW CAN I HELP:	
NOTES:	

Weekly PLANNER

MONDAY	TUESDAY	WEDNESDAY	THURSDAY

TO DO LIST:

- ☐
- ☐
- ☐
- ☐
- ☐
- ☐
- ☐
- ☐
- ☐
- ☐
- ☐
- ☐

APPOINTMENTS:

SPECIAL EVENTS:

SELF CARE AND HABIT TRACKER:

	M	T	W	T	F	S	S
	M	T	W	T	F	S	S
	M	T	W	T	F	S	S
	M	T	W	T	F	S	S
	M	T	W	T	F	S	S
	M	T	W	T	F	S	S
	M	T	W	T	F	S	S
	M	T	W	T	F	S	S

WEEK OF: ....

FRIDAY	SATURDAY	SUNDAY	REFLECTIONS:

WEEKLY GOALS:

....

....

....

....

....

....

ACTION PLAN:

MOTIVATION:

....

....

....

....

AFFIRMATIONS:

....

....

....

....

....

NOTES:

NEXT WEEK:

Power HOUR

DATE: ....

TOP PRIORITIES:

CALLS & CHECK-INS

FOLLOW-UPS

FIND NEW LEADS

CORRESPONDENCES

SOCIAL MEDIA POSTS

DATE: ....

TOP PRIORITIES:

CALLS & CHECK-INS

FOLLOW-UPS

FIND NEW LEADS

CORRESPONDENCES

SOCIAL MEDIA POSTS

Sales & Expense TRACKER

DATE	CUSTOMER	PRODUCT	QTY	AMOUNT	NOTES	✓

DATE	EXPENSE DESCRIPTION	AMOUNT	✓

Downline DEVELOPMENT

NAME:	DATE:

GOALS:

ACHIEVEMENTS:

FOCUS AREAS:

MOTIVATION:

NEXT MEETING:

NOTES:

NAME:	DATE:

GOALS:

ACHIEVEMENTS:

FOCUS AREAS:

MOTIVATION:

NEXT MEETING:

NOTES:

NAME:	DATE:

GOALS:

ACHIEVEMENTS:

FOCUS AREAS:

MOTIVATION:

NEXT MEETING:

NOTES:

Recruiting POTENTIALS

NAME:	FOLLOW-UP DATE:

THEIR WHY:
WHAT'S THE HOLD-UP:
HOW CAN I HELP:
NOTES:

NAME:	FOLLOW-UP DATE:

THEIR WHY:
WHAT'S THE HOLD-UP:
HOW CAN I HELP:
NOTES:

NAME:	FOLLOW-UP DATE:

THEIR WHY:
WHAT'S THE HOLD-UP:
HOW CAN I HELP:
NOTES:

NAME:	FOLLOW-UP DATE:

THEIR WHY:
WHAT'S THE HOLD-UP:
HOW CAN I HELP:
NOTES:

NAME:	FOLLOW-UP DATE:

THEIR WHY:
WHAT'S THE HOLD-UP:
HOW CAN I HELP:
NOTES:

Weekly PLANNER

MONDAY	TUESDAY	WEDNESDAY	THURSDAY

TO DO LIST:

- ☐
- ☐
- ☐
- ☐
- ☐
- ☐
- ☐
- ☐
- ☐
- ☐
- ☐
- ☐

APPOINTMENTS:

SPECIAL EVENTS:

SELF CARE AND HABIT TRACKER:

	M	T	W	T	F	S	S
	M	T	W	T	F	S	S
	M	T	W	T	F	S	S
	M	T	W	T	F	S	S
	M	T	W	T	F	S	S
	M	T	W	T	F	S	S
	M	T	W	T	F	S	S
	M	T	W	T	F	S	S

WEEK OF:

FRIDAY	SATURDAY	SUNDAY	REFLECTIONS:

WEEKLY GOALS:

ACTION PLAN:

MOTIVATION:

AFFIRMATIONS:

NOTES:

NEXT WEEK:

Power HOUR

DATE:	DATE:
TOP PRIORITIES:	**TOP PRIORITIES:**
CALLS & CHECK-INS	**CALLS & CHECK-INS**
FOLLOW-UPS	**FOLLOW-UPS**
FIND NEW LEADS	**FIND NEW LEADS**
CORRESPONDENCES	**CORRESPONDENCES**
SOCIAL MEDIA POSTS	**SOCIAL MEDIA POSTS**

Sales & Expense TRACKER

DATE	CUSTOMER	PRODUCT	QTY	AMOUNT	NOTES	✓

DATE	EXPENSE DESCRIPTION	AMOUNT	✓

Downline DEVELOPMENT

NAME:	DATE:

GOALS:

ACHIEVEMENTS:

FOCUS AREAS:

MOTIVATION:

NEXT MEETING:

NOTES:

NAME:	DATE:

GOALS:

ACHIEVEMENTS:

FOCUS AREAS:

MOTIVATION:

NEXT MEETING:

NOTES:

NAME:	DATE:

GOALS:

ACHIEVEMENTS:

FOCUS AREAS:

MOTIVATION:

NEXT MEETING:

NOTES:

Recruiting POTENTIALS

NAME: | **FOLLOW-UP DATE:**

THEIR WHY:

WHAT'S THE HOLD-UP:

HOW CAN I HELP:

NOTES:

NAME: | **FOLLOW-UP DATE:**

THEIR WHY:

WHAT'S THE HOLD-UP:

HOW CAN I HELP:

NOTES:

NAME: | **FOLLOW-UP DATE:**

THEIR WHY:

WHAT'S THE HOLD-UP:

HOW CAN I HELP:

NOTES:

NAME: | **FOLLOW-UP DATE:**

THEIR WHY:

WHAT'S THE HOLD-UP:

HOW CAN I HELP:

NOTES:

NAME: | **FOLLOW-UP DATE:**

THEIR WHY:

WHAT'S THE HOLD-UP:

HOW CAN I HELP:

NOTES:

Weekly PLANNER

MONDAY	TUESDAY	WEDNESDAY	THURSDAY

TO DO LIST:

- ☐
- ☐
- ☐
- ☐
- ☐
- ☐
- ☐
- ☐
- ☐
- ☐
- ☐
- ☐

APPOINTMENTS:

SPECIAL EVENTS:

SELF CARE AND HABIT TRACKER:

	M	T	W	T	F	S	S
	M	T	W	T	F	S	S
	M	T	W	T	F	S	S
	M	T	W	T	F	S	S
	M	T	W	T	F	S	S
	M	T	W	T	F	S	S
	M	T	W	T	F	S	S
	M	T	W	T	F	S	S

WEEK OF:

FRIDAY	SATURDAY	SUNDAY	REFLECTIONS:

WEEKLY GOALS:

ACTION PLAN:

MOTIVATION:

AFFIRMATIONS:

NOTES:

NEXT WEEK:

Power HOUR

DATE: ....

TOP PRIORITIES:

CALLS & CHECK-INS

FOLLOW-UPS

FIND NEW LEADS

CORRESPONDENCES

SOCIAL MEDIA POSTS

DATE: ....

TOP PRIORITIES:

CALLS & CHECK-INS

FOLLOW-UPS

FIND NEW LEADS

CORRESPONDENCES

SOCIAL MEDIA POSTS

Sales & Expense TRACKER

DATE	CUSTOMER	PRODUCT	QTY	AMOUNT	NOTES	✓

DATE	EXPENSE DESCRIPTION	AMOUNT	✓

Downline DEVELOPMENT

NAME:	DATE:

GOALS:

ACHIEVEMENTS:

FOCUS AREAS:

MOTIVATION:

NEXT MEETING:

NOTES:

NAME:	DATE:

GOALS:

ACHIEVEMENTS:

FOCUS AREAS:

MOTIVATION:

NEXT MEETING:

NOTES:

NAME:	DATE:

GOALS:

ACHIEVEMENTS:

FOCUS AREAS:

MOTIVATION:

NEXT MEETING:

NOTES:

Recruiting POTENTIALS

NAME:	FOLLOW-UP DATE:
THEIR WHY:	
WHAT'S THE HOLD-UP:	
HOW CAN I HELP:	
NOTES:	

NAME:	FOLLOW-UP DATE:
THEIR WHY:	
WHAT'S THE HOLD-UP:	
HOW CAN I HELP:	
NOTES:	

NAME:	FOLLOW-UP DATE:
THEIR WHY:	
WHAT'S THE HOLD-UP:	
HOW CAN I HELP:	
NOTES:	

NAME:	FOLLOW-UP DATE:
THEIR WHY:	
WHAT'S THE HOLD-UP:	
HOW CAN I HELP:	
NOTES:	

NAME:	FOLLOW-UP DATE:
THEIR WHY:	
WHAT'S THE HOLD-UP:	
HOW CAN I HELP:	
NOTES:	

Weekly PLANNER

MONDAY	TUESDAY	WEDNESDAY	THURSDAY

TO DO LIST:

- [ ]
- [ ]
- [ ]
- [ ]
- [ ]
- [ ]
- [ ]
- [ ]
- [ ]
- [ ]
- [ ]
- [ ]

APPOINTMENTS:

SPECIAL EVENTS:

SELF CARE AND HABIT TRACKER:

	M	T	W	T	F	S	S
	M	T	W	T	F	S	S
	M	T	W	T	F	S	S
	M	T	W	T	F	S	S
	M	T	W	T	F	S	S
	M	T	W	T	F	S	S
	M	T	W	T	F	S	S
	M	T	W	T	F	S	S
	M	T	W	T	F	S	S

WEEK OF:

FRIDAY	SATURDAY	SUNDAY	REFLECTIONS:

WEEKLY GOALS:

ACTION PLAN:

MOTIVATION:

AFFIRMATIONS:

NOTES:

NEXT WEEK:

Power HOUR

DATE: ....   DATE: ....

TOP PRIORITIES:

TOP PRIORITIES:

CALLS & CHECK-INS

CALLS & CHECK-INS

FOLLOW-UPS

FOLLOW-UPS

FIND NEW LEADS

FIND NEW LEADS

CORRESPONDENCES

CORRESPONDENCES

SOCIAL MEDIA POSTS

SOCIAL MEDIA POSTS

Sales & Expense TRACKER

DATE	CUSTOMER	PRODUCT	QTY	AMOUNT	NOTES	✓

DATE	EXPENSE DESCRIPTION	AMOUNT	✓

Downline DEVELOPMENT

NAME: | **DATE:**

GOALS:

ACHIEVEMENTS:

FOCUS AREAS:

MOTIVATION:

NEXT MEETING:

NOTES:

NAME: | **DATE:**

GOALS:

ACHIEVEMENTS:

FOCUS AREAS:

MOTIVATION:

NEXT MEETING:

NOTES:

NAME: | **DATE:**

GOALS:

ACHIEVEMENTS:

FOCUS AREAS:

MOTIVATION:

NEXT MEETING:

NOTES:

Recruiting POTENTIALS

NAME:	FOLLOW-UP DATE:

THEIR WHY:
WHAT'S THE HOLD-UP:
HOW CAN I HELP:
NOTES:

NAME:	FOLLOW-UP DATE:

THEIR WHY:
WHAT'S THE HOLD-UP:
HOW CAN I HELP:
NOTES:

NAME:	FOLLOW-UP DATE:

THEIR WHY:
WHAT'S THE HOLD-UP:
HOW CAN I HELP:
NOTES:

NAME:	FOLLOW-UP DATE:

THEIR WHY:
WHAT'S THE HOLD-UP:
HOW CAN I HELP:
NOTES:

NAME:	FOLLOW-UP DATE:

THEIR WHY:
WHAT'S THE HOLD-UP:
HOW CAN I HELP:
NOTES:

Weekly PLANNER

MONDAY	TUESDAY	WEDNESDAY	THURSDAY

TO DO LIST:

- ☐
- ☐
- ☐
- ☐
- ☐
- ☐
- ☐
- ☐
- ☐
- ☐
- ☐
- ☐

APPOINTMENTS:

SPECIAL EVENTS:

SELF CARE AND HABIT TRACKER:

	M	T	W	T	F	S	S
	M	T	W	T	F	S	S
	M	T	W	T	F	S	S
	M	T	W	T	F	S	S
	M	T	W	T	F	S	S
	M	T	W	T	F	S	S
	M	T	W	T	F	S	S
	M	T	W	T	F	S	S
	M	T	W	T	F	S	S

WEEK OF:

FRIDAY	SATURDAY	SUNDAY	REFLECTIONS:

WEEKLY GOALS:

ACTION PLAN:

MOTIVATION:

AFFIRMATIONS:

NOTES:

NEXT WEEK:

Power HOUR

DATE: ....

TOP PRIORITIES:

CALLS & CHECK-INS

FOLLOW-UPS

FIND NEW LEADS

CORRESPONDENCES

SOCIAL MEDIA POSTS

DATE: ....

TOP PRIORITIES:

CALLS & CHECK-INS

FOLLOW-UPS

FIND NEW LEADS

CORRESPONDENCES

SOCIAL MEDIA POSTS

Sales & Expense TRACKER

DATE	CUSTOMER	PRODUCT	QTY	AMOUNT	NOTES	✓

DATE	EXPENSE DESCRIPTION	AMOUNT	✓

Downline DEVELOPMENT

NAME:	DATE:

GOALS:

ACHIEVEMENTS:

FOCUS AREAS:

MOTIVATION:

NEXT MEETING:

NOTES:

NAME:	DATE:

GOALS:

ACHIEVEMENTS:

FOCUS AREAS:

MOTIVATION:

NEXT MEETING:

NOTES:

NAME:	DATE:

GOALS:

ACHIEVEMENTS:

FOCUS AREAS:

MOTIVATION:

NEXT MEETING:

NOTES:

Recruiting POTENTIALS

NAME: | **FOLLOW-UP DATE:**

THEIR WHY:

WHAT'S THE HOLD-UP:

HOW CAN I HELP:

NOTES:

NAME: | **FOLLOW-UP DATE:**

THEIR WHY:

WHAT'S THE HOLD-UP:

HOW CAN I HELP:

NOTES:

NAME: | **FOLLOW-UP DATE:**

THEIR WHY:

WHAT'S THE HOLD-UP:

HOW CAN I HELP:

NOTES:

NAME: | **FOLLOW-UP DATE:**

THEIR WHY:

WHAT'S THE HOLD-UP:

HOW CAN I HELP:

NOTES:

NAME: | **FOLLOW-UP DATE:**

THEIR WHY:

WHAT'S THE HOLD-UP:

HOW CAN I HELP:

NOTES:

Weekly PLANNER

MONDAY	TUESDAY	WEDNESDAY	THURSDAY

TO DO LIST:

- ☐
- ☐
- ☐
- ☐
- ☐
- ☐
- ☐
- ☐
- ☐
- ☐
- ☐
- ☐

APPOINTMENTS:

SPECIAL EVENTS:

SELF CARE AND HABIT TRACKER:

	M	T	W	T	F	S	S
	M	T	W	T	F	S	S
	M	T	W	T	F	S	S
	M	T	W	T	F	S	S
	M	T	W	T	F	S	S
	M	T	W	T	F	S	S
	M	T	W	T	F	S	S
	M	T	W	T	F	S	S

WEEK OF: ....

FRIDAY	SATURDAY	SUNDAY	REFLECTIONS:

WEEKLY GOALS:

ACTION PLAN:

MOTIVATION:

AFFIRMATIONS:

NOTES:

NEXT WEEK:

Power HOUR

DATE: ....

TOP PRIORITIES:

CALLS & CHECK-INS

FOLLOW-UPS

FIND NEW LEADS

CORRESPONDENCES

SOCIAL MEDIA POSTS

DATE: ....

TOP PRIORITIES:

CALLS & CHECK-INS

FOLLOW-UPS

FIND NEW LEADS

CORRESPONDENCES

SOCIAL MEDIA POSTS

Sales & Expense TRACKER

DATE	CUSTOMER	PRODUCT	QTY	AMOUNT	NOTES	✓

DATE	EXPENSE DESCRIPTION	AMOUNT	✓

Downline DEVELOPMENT

NAME: | **DATE:**

GOALS:

ACHIEVEMENTS:

FOCUS AREAS:

MOTIVATION:

NEXT MEETING:

NOTES:

NAME: | **DATE:**

GOALS:

ACHIEVEMENTS:

FOCUS AREAS:

MOTIVATION:

NEXT MEETING:

NOTES:

NAME: | **DATE:**

GOALS:

ACHIEVEMENTS:

FOCUS AREAS:

MOTIVATION:

NEXT MEETING:

NOTES:

Recruiting POTENTIALS

NAME:	FOLLOW-UP DATE:
THEIR WHY:	
WHAT'S THE HOLD-UP:	
HOW CAN I HELP:	
NOTES:	

NAME:	FOLLOW-UP DATE:
THEIR WHY:	
WHAT'S THE HOLD-UP:	
HOW CAN I HELP:	
NOTES:	

NAME:	FOLLOW-UP DATE:
THEIR WHY:	
WHAT'S THE HOLD-UP:	
HOW CAN I HELP:	
NOTES:	

NAME:	FOLLOW-UP DATE:
THEIR WHY:	
WHAT'S THE HOLD-UP:	
HOW CAN I HELP:	
NOTES:	

NAME:	FOLLOW-UP DATE:
THEIR WHY:	
WHAT'S THE HOLD-UP:	
HOW CAN I HELP:	
NOTES:	

Weekly PLANNER

MONDAY	TUESDAY	WEDNESDAY	THURSDAY

TO DO LIST:

- ☐
- ☐
- ☐
- ☐
- ☐
- ☐
- ☐
- ☐
- ☐
- ☐
- ☐
- ☐

APPOINTMENTS:

SPECIAL EVENTS:

SELF CARE AND HABIT TRACKER:

	M	T	W	T	F	S	S
	M	T	W	T	F	S	S
	M	T	W	T	F	S	S
	M	T	W	T	F	S	S
	M	T	W	T	F	S	S
	M	T	W	T	F	S	S
	M	T	W	T	F	S	S
	M	T	W	T	F	S	S
	M	T	W	T	F	S	S

WEEK OF: ....

FRIDAY	SATURDAY	SUNDAY	REFLECTIONS:

WEEKLY GOALS:

ACTION PLAN:

MOTIVATION:

AFFIRMATIONS:

NOTES:

NEXT WEEK:

Power HOUR

DATE: ....

DATE: ....

TOP PRIORITIES:	TOP PRIORITIES:

CALLS & CHECK-INS	CALLS & CHECK-INS

FOLLOW-UPS	FOLLOW-UPS

FIND NEW LEADS	FIND NEW LEADS

CORRESPONDENCES	CORRESPONDENCES

SOCIAL MEDIA POSTS	SOCIAL MEDIA POSTS

Sales & Expense TRACKER

DATE	CUSTOMER	PRODUCT	QTY	AMOUNT	NOTES	✓

DATE	EXPENSE DESCRIPTION	AMOUNT	✓

Downline DEVELOPMENT

NAME: | **DATE:**

GOALS:

ACHIEVEMENTS:

FOCUS AREAS:

MOTIVATION:

NEXT MEETING:

NOTES:

NAME: | **DATE:**

GOALS:

ACHIEVEMENTS:

FOCUS AREAS:

MOTIVATION:

NEXT MEETING:

NOTES:

NAME: | **DATE:**

GOALS:

ACHIEVEMENTS:

FOCUS AREAS:

MOTIVATION:

NEXT MEETING:

NOTES:

Recruiting POTENTIALS

NAME: | **FOLLOW-UP DATE:**
THEIR WHY:
WHAT'S THE HOLD-UP:
HOW CAN I HELP:
NOTES:

NAME: | **FOLLOW-UP DATE:**
THEIR WHY:
WHAT'S THE HOLD-UP:
HOW CAN I HELP:
NOTES:

NAME: | **FOLLOW-UP DATE:**
THEIR WHY:
WHAT'S THE HOLD-UP:
HOW CAN I HELP:
NOTES:

NAME: | **FOLLOW-UP DATE:**
THEIR WHY:
WHAT'S THE HOLD-UP:
HOW CAN I HELP:
NOTES:

NAME: | **FOLLOW-UP DATE:**
THEIR WHY:
WHAT'S THE HOLD-UP:
HOW CAN I HELP:
NOTES:

Weekly PLANNER

MONDAY	TUESDAY	WEDNESDAY	THURSDAY

TO DO LIST:

- ☐
- ☐
- ☐
- ☐
- ☐
- ☐
- ☐
- ☐
- ☐
- ☐
- ☐
- ☐

APPOINTMENTS:

SPECIAL EVENTS:

SELF CARE AND HABIT TRACKER:

	M	T	W	T	F	S	S
	M	T	W	T	F	S	S
	M	T	W	T	F	S	S
	M	T	W	T	F	S	S
	M	T	W	T	F	S	S
	M	T	W	T	F	S	S
	M	T	W	T	F	S	S
	M	T	W	T	F	S	S

WEEK OF:

FRIDAY	SATURDAY	SUNDAY	REFLECTIONS:

WEEKLY GOALS:

ACTION PLAN:

MOTIVATION:

AFFIRMATIONS:

NOTES:

NEXT WEEK:

Power HOUR

DATE: ....

TOP PRIORITIES:

DATE: ....

TOP PRIORITIES:

CALLS & CHECK-INS

CALLS & CHECK-INS

FOLLOW-UPS

FOLLOW-UPS

FIND NEW LEADS

FIND NEW LEADS

CORRESPONDENCES

CORRESPONDENCES

SOCIAL MEDIA POSTS

SOCIAL MEDIA POSTS

Sales & Expense TRACKER

DATE	CUSTOMER	PRODUCT	QTY	AMOUNT	NOTES	✓

DATE	EXPENSE DESCRIPTION	AMOUNT	✓

Downline DEVELOPMENT

NAME: | **DATE:**

GOALS:

ACHIEVEMENTS:

FOCUS AREAS:

MOTIVATION:

NEXT MEETING:

NOTES:

NAME: | **DATE:**

GOALS:

ACHIEVEMENTS:

FOCUS AREAS:

MOTIVATION:

NEXT MEETING:

NOTES:

NAME: | **DATE:**

GOALS:

ACHIEVEMENTS:

FOCUS AREAS:

MOTIVATION:

NEXT MEETING:

NOTES:

Recruiting POTENTIALS

NAME:	FOLLOW-UP DATE:
THEIR WHY:	
WHAT'S THE HOLD-UP:	
HOW CAN I HELP:	
NOTES:	

NAME:	FOLLOW-UP DATE:
THEIR WHY:	
WHAT'S THE HOLD-UP:	
HOW CAN I HELP:	
NOTES:	

NAME:	FOLLOW-UP DATE:
THEIR WHY:	
WHAT'S THE HOLD-UP:	
HOW CAN I HELP:	
NOTES:	

NAME:	FOLLOW-UP DATE:
THEIR WHY:	
WHAT'S THE HOLD-UP:	
HOW CAN I HELP:	
NOTES:	

NAME:	FOLLOW-UP DATE:
THEIR WHY:	
WHAT'S THE HOLD-UP:	
HOW CAN I HELP:	
NOTES:	

Weekly PLANNER

MONDAY	TUESDAY	WEDNESDAY	THURSDAY

TO DO LIST:

- ☐
- ☐
- ☐
- ☐
- ☐
- ☐
- ☐
- ☐
- ☐
- ☐
- ☐
- ☐

APPOINTMENTS:

SPECIAL EVENTS:

SELF CARE AND HABIT TRACKER:

	M	T	W	T	F	S	S
	M	T	W	T	F	S	S
	M	T	W	T	F	S	S
	M	T	W	T	F	S	S
	M	T	W	T	F	S	S
	M	T	W	T	F	S	S
	M	T	W	T	F	S	S
	M	T	W	T	F	S	S

WEEK OF: ....

FRIDAY	SATURDAY	SUNDAY	REFLECTIONS:

WEEKLY GOALS:

ACTION PLAN:

MOTIVATION:

AFFIRMATIONS:

NOTES:

NEXT WEEK:

Power HOUR

DATE: ....

TOP PRIORITIES:

DATE: ....

TOP PRIORITIES:

CALLS & CHECK-INS

CALLS & CHECK-INS

FOLLOW-UPS

FOLLOW-UPS

FIND NEW LEADS

FIND NEW LEADS

CORRESPONDENCES

CORRESPONDENCES

SOCIAL MEDIA POSTS

SOCIAL MEDIA POSTS

Sales & Expense TRACKER

DATE	CUSTOMER	PRODUCT	QTY	AMOUNT	NOTES	✓

DATE	EXPENSE DESCRIPTION	AMOUNT	✓

Downline DEVELOPMENT

NAME:	DATE:

GOALS:

ACHIEVEMENTS:

FOCUS AREAS:

MOTIVATION:

NEXT MEETING:

NOTES:

NAME:	DATE:

GOALS:

ACHIEVEMENTS:

FOCUS AREAS:

MOTIVATION:

NEXT MEETING:

NOTES:

NAME:	DATE:

GOALS:

ACHIEVEMENTS:

FOCUS AREAS:

MOTIVATION:

NEXT MEETING:

NOTES:

Recruiting POTENTIALS

NAME:	FOLLOW-UP DATE:
THEIR WHY:	
WHAT'S THE HOLD-UP:	
HOW CAN I HELP:	
NOTES:	

NAME:	FOLLOW-UP DATE:
THEIR WHY:	
WHAT'S THE HOLD-UP:	
HOW CAN I HELP:	
NOTES:	

NAME:	FOLLOW-UP DATE:
THEIR WHY:	
WHAT'S THE HOLD-UP:	
HOW CAN I HELP:	
NOTES:	

NAME:	FOLLOW-UP DATE:
THEIR WHY:	
WHAT'S THE HOLD-UP:	
HOW CAN I HELP:	
NOTES:	

NAME:	FOLLOW-UP DATE:
THEIR WHY:	
WHAT'S THE HOLD-UP:	
HOW CAN I HELP:	
NOTES:	

Weekly PLANNER

MONDAY	TUESDAY	WEDNESDAY	THURSDAY

TO DO LIST:

- [ ]
- [ ]
- [ ]
- [ ]
- [ ]
- [ ]
- [ ]
- [ ]
- [ ]
- [ ]
- [ ]
- [ ]

APPOINTMENTS:

SPECIAL EVENTS:

SELF CARE AND HABIT TRACKER:

	M	T	W	T	F	S	S
	M	T	W	T	F	S	S
	M	T	W	T	F	S	S
	M	T	W	T	F	S	S
	M	T	W	T	F	S	S
	M	T	W	T	F	S	S
	M	T	W	T	F	S	S
	M	T	W	T	F	S	S

WEEK OF:

FRIDAY	SATURDAY	SUNDAY	REFLECTIONS:

WEEKLY GOALS:

ACTION PLAN:

MOTIVATION:

AFFIRMATIONS:

NOTES:

NEXT WEEK:

Power HOUR

DATE: ....

TOP PRIORITIES:

DATE: ....

TOP PRIORITIES:

CALLS & CHECK-INS

CALLS & CHECK-INS

FOLLOW-UPS

FOLLOW-UPS

FIND NEW LEADS

FIND NEW LEADS

CORRESPONDENCES

CORRESPONDENCES

SOCIAL MEDIA POSTS

SOCIAL MEDIA POSTS

Sales & Expense TRACKER

DATE	CUSTOMER	PRODUCT	QTY	AMOUNT	NOTES	✓

DATE	EXPENSE DESCRIPTION	AMOUNT	✓

Downline DEVELOPMENT

NAME:	DATE:

GOALS:

ACHIEVEMENTS:

FOCUS AREAS:

MOTIVATION:

NEXT MEETING:

NOTES:

NAME:	DATE:

GOALS:

ACHIEVEMENTS:

FOCUS AREAS:

MOTIVATION:

NEXT MEETING:

NOTES:

NAME:	DATE:

GOALS:

ACHIEVEMENTS:

FOCUS AREAS:

MOTIVATION:

NEXT MEETING:

NOTES:

Recruiting POTENTIALS

NAME:	FOLLOW-UP DATE:
THEIR WHY:	
WHAT'S THE HOLD-UP:	
HOW CAN I HELP:	
NOTES:	

NAME:	FOLLOW-UP DATE:
THEIR WHY:	
WHAT'S THE HOLD-UP:	
HOW CAN I HELP:	
NOTES:	

NAME:	FOLLOW-UP DATE:
THEIR WHY:	
WHAT'S THE HOLD-UP:	
HOW CAN I HELP:	
NOTES:	

NAME:	FOLLOW-UP DATE:
THEIR WHY:	
WHAT'S THE HOLD-UP:	
HOW CAN I HELP:	
NOTES:	

NAME:	FOLLOW-UP DATE:
THEIR WHY:	
WHAT'S THE HOLD-UP:	
HOW CAN I HELP:	
NOTES:	

Weekly PLANNER

MONDAY	TUESDAY	WEDNESDAY	THURSDAY

TO DO LIST:

- ☐
- ☐
- ☐
- ☐
- ☐
- ☐
- ☐
- ☐
- ☐
- ☐
- ☐
- ☐

APPOINTMENTS:

SPECIAL EVENTS:

SELF CARE AND HABIT TRACKER:

	M	T	W	T	F	S	S
	M	T	W	T	F	S	S
	M	T	W	T	F	S	S
	M	T	W	T	F	S	S
	M	T	W	T	F	S	S
	M	T	W	T	F	S	S
	M	T	W	T	F	S	S
	M	T	W	T	F	S	S

WEEK OF:

FRIDAY	SATURDAY	SUNDAY	REFLECTIONS:

WEEKLY GOALS:

ACTION PLAN:

MOTIVATION:

AFFIRMATIONS:

NOTES:

NEXT WEEK:

Power HOUR

DATE: ....

TOP PRIORITIES:

DATE: ....

TOP PRIORITIES:

CALLS & CHECK-INS

CALLS & CHECK-INS

FOLLOW-UPS

FOLLOW-UPS

FIND NEW LEADS

FIND NEW LEADS

CORRESPONDENCES

CORRESPONDENCES

SOCIAL MEDIA POSTS

SOCIAL MEDIA POSTS

Sales & Expense TRACKER

DATE	CUSTOMER	PRODUCT	QTY	AMOUNT	NOTES	✓

DATE	EXPENSE DESCRIPTION	AMOUNT	✓

Downline DEVELOPMENT

NAME:	DATE:

GOALS:

ACHIEVEMENTS:

FOCUS AREAS:

MOTIVATION:

NEXT MEETING:

NOTES:

NAME:	DATE:

GOALS:

ACHIEVEMENTS:

FOCUS AREAS:

MOTIVATION:

NEXT MEETING:

NOTES:

NAME:	DATE:

GOALS:

ACHIEVEMENTS:

FOCUS AREAS:

MOTIVATION:

NEXT MEETING:

NOTES:

Recruiting POTENTIALS

NAME:	FOLLOW-UP DATE:

THEIR WHY:

WHAT'S THE HOLD-UP:

HOW CAN I HELP:

NOTES:

NAME:	FOLLOW-UP DATE:

THEIR WHY:

WHAT'S THE HOLD-UP:

HOW CAN I HELP:

NOTES:

NAME:	FOLLOW-UP DATE:

THEIR WHY:

WHAT'S THE HOLD-UP:

HOW CAN I HELP:

NOTES:

NAME:	FOLLOW-UP DATE:

THEIR WHY:

WHAT'S THE HOLD-UP:

HOW CAN I HELP:

NOTES:

NAME:	FOLLOW-UP DATE:

THEIR WHY:

WHAT'S THE HOLD-UP:

HOW CAN I HELP:

NOTES:

Weekly PLANNER

MONDAY	TUESDAY	WEDNESDAY	THURSDAY

TO DO LIST:

- ☐
- ☐
- ☐
- ☐
- ☐
- ☐
- ☐
- ☐
- ☐
- ☐
- ☐
- ☐

APPOINTMENTS:

SPECIAL EVENTS:

SELF CARE AND HABIT TRACKER:

	M	T	W	T	F	S	S
	M	T	W	T	F	S	S
	M	T	W	T	F	S	S
	M	T	W	T	F	S	S
	M	T	W	T	F	S	S
	M	T	W	T	F	S	S
	M	T	W	T	F	S	S
	M	T	W	T	F	S	S

WEEK OF: ....

FRIDAY	SATURDAY	SUNDAY	REFLECTIONS:

WEEKLY GOALS:

....
....
....
....
....
....

ACTION PLAN:

MOTIVATION:

....
....
....
....

AFFIRMATIONS:

....
....
....
....
....

NOTES:

NEXT WEEK:

Power HOUR

DATE: ....

TOP PRIORITIES:

CALLS & CHECK-INS

FOLLOW-UPS

FIND NEW LEADS

CORRESPONDENCES

SOCIAL MEDIA POSTS

DATE: ....

TOP PRIORITIES:

CALLS & CHECK-INS

FOLLOW-UPS

FIND NEW LEADS

CORRESPONDENCES

SOCIAL MEDIA POSTS

Sales & Expense TRACKER

DATE	CUSTOMER	PRODUCT	QTY	AMOUNT	NOTES	✓

DATE	EXPENSE DESCRIPTION	AMOUNT	✓

Downline DEVELOPMENT

NAME: | **DATE:**

GOALS:

ACHIEVEMENTS:

FOCUS AREAS:

MOTIVATION:

NEXT MEETING:

NOTES:

NAME: | **DATE:**

GOALS:

ACHIEVEMENTS:

FOCUS AREAS:

MOTIVATION:

NEXT MEETING:

NOTES:

NAME: | **DATE:**

GOALS:

ACHIEVEMENTS:

FOCUS AREAS:

MOTIVATION:

NEXT MEETING:

NOTES:

Recruiting POTENTIALS

NAME:	FOLLOW-UP DATE:

THEIR WHY:

WHAT'S THE HOLD-UP:

HOW CAN I HELP:

NOTES:

NAME:	FOLLOW-UP DATE:

THEIR WHY:

WHAT'S THE HOLD-UP:

HOW CAN I HELP:

NOTES:

NAME:	FOLLOW-UP DATE:

THEIR WHY:

WHAT'S THE HOLD-UP:

HOW CAN I HELP:

NOTES:

NAME:	FOLLOW-UP DATE:

THEIR WHY:

WHAT'S THE HOLD-UP:

HOW CAN I HELP:

NOTES:

NAME:	FOLLOW-UP DATE:

THEIR WHY:

WHAT'S THE HOLD-UP:

HOW CAN I HELP:

NOTES:

Weekly PLANNER

MONDAY	TUESDAY	WEDNESDAY	THURSDAY

TO DO LIST:

☐
☐
☐
☐
☐
☐
☐
☐
☐
☐
☐
☐

APPOINTMENTS:

SPECIAL EVENTS:

SELF CARE AND HABIT TRACKER:

	M	T	W	T	F	S	S
	M	T	W	T	F	S	S
	M	T	W	T	F	S	S
	M	T	W	T	F	S	S
	M	T	W	T	F	S	S
	M	T	W	T	F	S	S
	M	T	W	T	F	S	S
	M	T	W	T	F	S	S

WEEK OF:

FRIDAY	SATURDAY	SUNDAY	REFLECTIONS:

WEEKLY GOALS:

ACTION PLAN:

MOTIVATION:

AFFIRMATIONS:

NOTES:

NEXT WEEK:

Power HOUR

DATE: ....

TOP PRIORITIES:

DATE: ....

TOP PRIORITIES:

CALLS & CHECK-INS

CALLS & CHECK-INS

FOLLOW-UPS

FOLLOW-UPS

FIND NEW LEADS

FIND NEW LEADS

CORRESPONDENCES

CORRESPONDENCES

SOCIAL MEDIA POSTS

SOCIAL MEDIA POSTS

Sales & Expense TRACKER

DATE	CUSTOMER	PRODUCT	QTY	AMOUNT	NOTES	✓

DATE	EXPENSE DESCRIPTION	AMOUNT	✓

Downline DEVELOPMENT

NAME:	DATE:

GOALS:

ACHIEVEMENTS:

FOCUS AREAS:

MOTIVATION:

NEXT MEETING:

NOTES:

NAME:	DATE:

GOALS:

ACHIEVEMENTS:

FOCUS AREAS:

MOTIVATION:

NEXT MEETING:

NOTES:

NAME:	DATE:

GOALS:

ACHIEVEMENTS:

FOCUS AREAS:

MOTIVATION:

NEXT MEETING:

NOTES:

Recruiting POTENTIALS

NAME: | **FOLLOW-UP DATE:**

THEIR WHY:

WHAT'S THE HOLD-UP:

HOW CAN I HELP:

NOTES:

NAME: | **FOLLOW-UP DATE:**

THEIR WHY:

WHAT'S THE HOLD-UP:

HOW CAN I HELP:

NOTES:

NAME: | **FOLLOW-UP DATE:**

THEIR WHY:

WHAT'S THE HOLD-UP:

HOW CAN I HELP:

NOTES:

NAME: | **FOLLOW-UP DATE:**

THEIR WHY:

WHAT'S THE HOLD-UP:

HOW CAN I HELP:

NOTES:

NAME: | **FOLLOW-UP DATE:**

THEIR WHY:

WHAT'S THE HOLD-UP:

HOW CAN I HELP:

NOTES:

Weekly PLANNER

MONDAY	TUESDAY	WEDNESDAY	THURSDAY

TO DO LIST:

☐
☐
☐
☐
☐
☐
☐
☐
☐
☐
☐
☐

APPOINTMENTS:

SPECIAL EVENTS:

SELF CARE AND HABIT TRACKER:

	M	T	W	T	F	S	S
	M	T	W	T	F	S	S
	M	T	W	T	F	S	S
	M	T	W	T	F	S	S
	M	T	W	T	F	S	S
	M	T	W	T	F	S	S
	M	T	W	T	F	S	S
	M	T	W	T	F	S	S

WEEK OF:

FRIDAY	SATURDAY	SUNDAY	REFLECTIONS:

WEEKLY GOALS:

ACTION PLAN:

MOTIVATION:

AFFIRMATIONS:

NOTES:

NEXT WEEK:

Power HOUR

DATE: ....   DATE: ....

TOP PRIORITIES:	TOP PRIORITIES:

CALLS & CHECK-INS	CALLS & CHECK-INS

FOLLOW-UPS	FOLLOW-UPS

FIND NEW LEADS	FIND NEW LEADS

CORRESPONDENCES	CORRESPONDENCES

SOCIAL MEDIA POSTS	SOCIAL MEDIA POSTS

Sales & Expense TRACKER

DATE	CUSTOMER	PRODUCT	QTY	AMOUNT	NOTES	✓

DATE	EXPENSE DESCRIPTION	AMOUNT	✓

Downline DEVELOPMENT

NAME:	DATE:

GOALS:

ACHIEVEMENTS:

FOCUS AREAS:

MOTIVATION:

NEXT MEETING:

NOTES:

NAME:	DATE:

GOALS:

ACHIEVEMENTS:

FOCUS AREAS:

MOTIVATION:

NEXT MEETING:

NOTES:

NAME:	DATE:

GOALS:

ACHIEVEMENTS:

FOCUS AREAS:

MOTIVATION:

NEXT MEETING:

NOTES:

Recruiting POTENTIALS

NAME:	FOLLOW-UP DATE:
THEIR WHY:	
WHAT'S THE HOLD-UP:	
HOW CAN I HELP:	
NOTES:	

NAME:	FOLLOW-UP DATE:
THEIR WHY:	
WHAT'S THE HOLD-UP:	
HOW CAN I HELP:	
NOTES:	

NAME:	FOLLOW-UP DATE:
THEIR WHY:	
WHAT'S THE HOLD-UP:	
HOW CAN I HELP:	
NOTES:	

NAME:	FOLLOW-UP DATE:
THEIR WHY:	
WHAT'S THE HOLD-UP:	
HOW CAN I HELP:	
NOTES:	

NAME:	FOLLOW-UP DATE:
THEIR WHY:	
WHAT'S THE HOLD-UP:	
HOW CAN I HELP:	
NOTES:	

Weekly PLANNER

MONDAY	TUESDAY	WEDNESDAY	THURSDAY

TO DO LIST:

- ☐
- ☐
- ☐
- ☐
- ☐
- ☐
- ☐
- ☐
- ☐
- ☐
- ☐
- ☐

APPOINTMENTS:

SPECIAL EVENTS:

SELF CARE AND HABIT TRACKER:

	M	T	W	T	F	S	S
	M	T	W	T	F	S	S
	M	T	W	T	F	S	S
	M	T	W	T	F	S	S
	M	T	W	T	F	S	S
	M	T	W	T	F	S	S
	M	T	W	T	F	S	S
	M	T	W	T	F	S	S
	M	T	W	T	F	S	S

WEEK OF:

FRIDAY	SATURDAY	SUNDAY	REFLECTIONS:

WEEKLY GOALS:

ACTION PLAN:

MOTIVATION:

AFFIRMATIONS:

NOTES:

NEXT WEEK:

Power **HOUR**

DATE: ....

TOP PRIORITIES:

CALLS & CHECK-INS

FOLLOW-UPS

FIND NEW LEADS

CORRESPONDENCES

SOCIAL MEDIA POSTS

DATE: ....

TOP PRIORITIES:

CALLS & CHECK-INS

FOLLOW-UPS

FIND NEW LEADS

CORRESPONDENCES

SOCIAL MEDIA POSTS

Sales & Expense TRACKER

DATE	CUSTOMER	PRODUCT	QTY	AMOUNT	NOTES	✓

DATE	EXPENSE DESCRIPTION	AMOUNT	✓

Downline DEVELOPMENT

NAME: | **DATE:**

GOALS:

ACHIEVEMENTS:

FOCUS AREAS:

MOTIVATION:

NEXT MEETING:

NOTES:

NAME: | **DATE:**

GOALS:

ACHIEVEMENTS:

FOCUS AREAS:

MOTIVATION:

NEXT MEETING:

NOTES:

NAME: | **DATE:**

GOALS:

ACHIEVEMENTS:

FOCUS AREAS:

MOTIVATION:

NEXT MEETING:

NOTES:

Recruiting POTENTIALS

NAME:	FOLLOW-UP DATE:
THEIR WHY:	
WHAT'S THE HOLD-UP:	
HOW CAN I HELP:	
NOTES:	

NAME:	FOLLOW-UP DATE:
THEIR WHY:	
WHAT'S THE HOLD-UP:	
HOW CAN I HELP:	
NOTES:	

NAME:	FOLLOW-UP DATE:
THEIR WHY:	
WHAT'S THE HOLD-UP:	
HOW CAN I HELP:	
NOTES:	

NAME:	FOLLOW-UP DATE:
THEIR WHY:	
WHAT'S THE HOLD-UP:	
HOW CAN I HELP:	
NOTES:	

NAME:	FOLLOW-UP DATE:
THEIR WHY:	
WHAT'S THE HOLD-UP:	
HOW CAN I HELP:	
NOTES:	

Weekly **PLANNER**

MONDAY	TUESDAY	WEDNESDAY	THURSDAY

TO DO LIST:

☐
☐
☐
☐
☐
☐
☐
☐
☐
☐
☐
☐

APPOINTMENTS:

SPECIAL EVENTS:

SELF CARE AND HABIT TRACKER:

	M	T	W	T	F	S	S
	M	T	W	T	F	S	S
	M	T	W	T	F	S	S
	M	T	W	T	F	S	S
	M	T	W	T	F	S	S
	M	T	W	T	F	S	S
	M	T	W	T	F	S	S
	M	T	W	T	F	S	S

WEEK OF:

FRIDAY	SATURDAY	SUNDAY	REFLECTIONS:

WEEKLY GOALS:

ACTION PLAN:

MOTIVATION:

AFFIRMATIONS:

NOTES:

NEXT WEEK:

Power **HOUR**

DATE: ....

TOP PRIORITIES:

CALLS & CHECK-INS

FOLLOW-UPS

FIND NEW LEADS

CORRESPONDENCES

SOCIAL MEDIA POSTS

DATE: ....

TOP PRIORITIES:

CALLS & CHECK-INS

FOLLOW-UPS

FIND NEW LEADS

CORRESPONDENCES

SOCIAL MEDIA POSTS

Sales & Expense TRACKER

DATE	CUSTOMER	PRODUCT	QTY	AMOUNT	NOTES	✓

DATE	EXPENSE DESCRIPTION	AMOUNT	✓

Downline DEVELOPMENT

NAME:	DATE:

GOALS:

ACHIEVEMENTS:

FOCUS AREAS:

MOTIVATION:

NEXT MEETING:

NOTES:

NAME:	DATE:

GOALS:

ACHIEVEMENTS:

FOCUS AREAS:

MOTIVATION:

NEXT MEETING:

NOTES:

NAME:	DATE:

GOALS:

ACHIEVEMENTS:

FOCUS AREAS:

MOTIVATION:

NEXT MEETING:

NOTES:

Recruiting POTENTIALS

NAME: | **FOLLOW-UP DATE:**

THEIR WHY:

WHAT'S THE HOLD-UP:

HOW CAN I HELP:

NOTES:

NAME: | **FOLLOW-UP DATE:**

THEIR WHY:

WHAT'S THE HOLD-UP:

HOW CAN I HELP:

NOTES:

NAME: | **FOLLOW-UP DATE:**

THEIR WHY:

WHAT'S THE HOLD-UP:

HOW CAN I HELP:

NOTES:

NAME: | **FOLLOW-UP DATE:**

THEIR WHY:

WHAT'S THE HOLD-UP:

HOW CAN I HELP:

NOTES:

NAME: | **FOLLOW-UP DATE:**

THEIR WHY:

WHAT'S THE HOLD-UP:

HOW CAN I HELP:

NOTES:

Weekly PLANNER

MONDAY	TUESDAY	WEDNESDAY	THURSDAY

TO DO LIST:

☐
☐
☐
☐
☐
☐
☐
☐
☐
☐
☐
☐

APPOINTMENTS:

SPECIAL EVENTS:

SELF CARE AND HABIT TRACKER:

	M	T	W	T	F	S	S
	M	T	W	T	F	S	S
	M	T	W	T	F	S	S
	M	T	W	T	F	S	S
	M	T	W	T	F	S	S
	M	T	W	T	F	S	S
	M	T	W	T	F	S	S
	M	T	W	T	F	S	S

WEEK OF:

FRIDAY	SATURDAY	SUNDAY	REFLECTIONS:

WEEKLY GOALS:

ACTION PLAN:

MOTIVATION:

AFFIRMATIONS:

NOTES:

NEXT WEEK:

Power HOUR

DATE: ....

TOP PRIORITIES:

CALLS & CHECK-INS

FOLLOW-UPS

FIND NEW LEADS

CORRESPONDENCES

SOCIAL MEDIA POSTS

DATE: ....

TOP PRIORITIES:

CALLS & CHECK-INS

FOLLOW-UPS

FIND NEW LEADS

CORRESPONDENCES

SOCIAL MEDIA POSTS

Sales & Expense TRACKER

DATE	CUSTOMER	PRODUCT	QTY	AMOUNT	NOTES	✓

DATE	EXPENSE DESCRIPTION	AMOUNT	✓

Downline DEVELOPMENT

NAME: | **DATE:**

GOALS:

ACHIEVEMENTS:

FOCUS AREAS:

MOTIVATION:

NEXT MEETING:

NOTES:

NAME: | **DATE:**

GOALS:

ACHIEVEMENTS:

FOCUS AREAS:

MOTIVATION:

NEXT MEETING:

NOTES:

NAME: | **DATE:**

GOALS:

ACHIEVEMENTS:

FOCUS AREAS:

MOTIVATION:

NEXT MEETING:

NOTES:

Recruiting POTENTIALS

NAME:	FOLLOW-UP DATE:
THEIR WHY:	
WHAT'S THE HOLD-UP:	
HOW CAN I HELP:	
NOTES:	

NAME:	FOLLOW-UP DATE:
THEIR WHY:	
WHAT'S THE HOLD-UP:	
HOW CAN I HELP:	
NOTES:	

NAME:	FOLLOW-UP DATE:
THEIR WHY:	
WHAT'S THE HOLD-UP:	
HOW CAN I HELP:	
NOTES:	

NAME:	FOLLOW-UP DATE:
THEIR WHY:	
WHAT'S THE HOLD-UP:	
HOW CAN I HELP:	
NOTES:	

NAME:	FOLLOW-UP DATE:
THEIR WHY:	
WHAT'S THE HOLD-UP:	
HOW CAN I HELP:	
NOTES:	

Weekly PLANNER

MONDAY	TUESDAY	WEDNESDAY	THURSDAY

TO DO LIST:

- ☐
- ☐
- ☐
- ☐
- ☐
- ☐
- ☐
- ☐
- ☐
- ☐
- ☐
- ☐

APPOINTMENTS:

SPECIAL EVENTS:

SELF CARE AND HABIT TRACKER:

	M	T	W	T	F	S	S
	M	T	W	T	F	S	S
	M	T	W	T	F	S	S
	M	T	W	T	F	S	S
	M	T	W	T	F	S	S
	M	T	W	T	F	S	S
	M	T	W	T	F	S	S
	M	T	W	T	F	S	S

WEEK OF:

FRIDAY	SATURDAY	SUNDAY	REFLECTIONS:

WEEKLY GOALS:

ACTION PLAN:

MOTIVATION:

AFFIRMATIONS:

NOTES:

NEXT WEEK:

Power HOUR

DATE: ....

DATE: ....

TOP PRIORITIES:

TOP PRIORITIES:

CALLS & CHECK-INS

CALLS & CHECK-INS

FOLLOW-UPS

FOLLOW-UPS

FIND NEW LEADS

FIND NEW LEADS

CORRESPONDENCES

CORRESPONDENCES

SOCIAL MEDIA POSTS

SOCIAL MEDIA POSTS

Sales & Expense TRACKER

DATE	CUSTOMER	PRODUCT	QTY	AMOUNT	NOTES	✓

DATE	EXPENSE DESCRIPTION	AMOUNT	✓

Downline DEVELOPMENT

NAME:	DATE:

GOALS:

ACHIEVEMENTS:

FOCUS AREAS:

MOTIVATION:

NEXT MEETING:

NOTES:

NAME:	DATE:

GOALS:

ACHIEVEMENTS:

FOCUS AREAS:

MOTIVATION:

NEXT MEETING:

NOTES:

NAME:	DATE:

GOALS:

ACHIEVEMENTS:

FOCUS AREAS:

MOTIVATION:

NEXT MEETING:

NOTES:

Recruiting POTENTIALS

NAME: | **FOLLOW-UP DATE:**

THEIR WHY:
WHAT'S THE HOLD-UP:
HOW CAN I HELP:
NOTES:

NAME: | **FOLLOW-UP DATE:**

THEIR WHY:
WHAT'S THE HOLD-UP:
HOW CAN I HELP:
NOTES:

NAME: | **FOLLOW-UP DATE:**

THEIR WHY:
WHAT'S THE HOLD-UP:
HOW CAN I HELP:
NOTES:

NAME: | **FOLLOW-UP DATE:**

THEIR WHY:
WHAT'S THE HOLD-UP:
HOW CAN I HELP:
NOTES:

NAME: | **FOLLOW-UP DATE:**

THEIR WHY:
WHAT'S THE HOLD-UP:
HOW CAN I HELP:
NOTES:

Made in the USA
Las Vegas, NV
27 October 2024